On a
Farm

by **Dana Meachen Rau**

Reading Consultant: Nanci R. Vargus, Ed.D.

Marshall Cavendish
Benchmark
New York

Picture Words

 basket

 corn

 cow

 eggs

 farm

 hay

 horse

 pumpkin

 sheep

 wagon

We can have fun on

a .

We can sit on in a .

We can pick a big 🎃.

We can milk the .

We can put in a .

We can pet the .

We can hide in the .

We can ride on a .

The  is fun.

20

Words to Know

hide
   to go where no one can see you

ride
   to be carried on something

Find Out More

Books

Adamson, Heather. *A Day in the Life of a Farmer*. Mankato, MN: Capstone Press, 2004.

Peterson, Cris. *Fantastic Farm Machines*. Honesdale, PA: Boyds Mills Press, 2006.

Wolfman, Judy. *Life on a Dairy Farm*. Minneapolis, MN: Carolrhoda Books, 2004.

Videos

Chater, Andrew. *A Trip to the Farm, Zoo, Seaside*. American Home Treasure.

Lancit Media Productions. *Let's Go to the Farm*. Goodtimes Home Video.

Web Sites

Corn Mazes America
http://www.cornmazesamerica.com/

The Farm and Farm Animals at Enchanted Learning
http://www.enchantedlearning.com/themes/farmanimals.shtml

Moo Milk
http://www.moomilk.com/

About the Author

Dana Meachen Rau is an author, editor, and illustrator. A graduate of Trinity College in Hartford, Connecticut, she has written more than one hundred books for children, including nonfiction, biographies, early readers, and historical fiction. She likes to go to her local farm to see the llamas near her home in Burlington, Connecticut.

About the Reading Consultant

Nanci R. Vargus, Ed.D., wants all children to enjoy reading. She used to teach first grade. Now she works at the University of Indianapolis. Nanci helps young people become teachers. She and her niece Kendra spent the weekend on a farm built in 1886 at the Conner Prairie Living History Museum in Fishers, Indiana.

Marshall Cavendish Benchmark
99 White Plains Road
Tarrytown, NY 10591-9001
www.marshallcavendish.us

All Internet addresses were correct at the time of printing.

Library of Congress Cataloging-In-Publication Data

Rau, Dana Meachen, 1971–
On a Farm / by Dana Meachen Rau.
    p. cm. — (Benchmark rebus)
Summary: Easy-to-read text with rubuses explores fun activities on a farm.
ISBN-13: 987-0-7614-2605-9
1. Rebuses. [1. Farm life—fiction. 2. Rebuses.] I. Title.
PZ7.R193975 Omw 2007
[E]—dc22   2006025350

Editor: Christine Florie
Publisher: Michelle Bisson
Art Director: Anahid Hamparian
Series Designer: Virginia Pope

Photo research by Connie Gardner

Rebus images, with the exception of the farm and cow, provided courtesy of *Dorling Kindersley*.

Cover photo by John Mielcarek/Dembinsky Photo Associates

The photographs in this book are used with permission and through the courtesy of:
Superstock: p. 2 (cow) age footstock; *Corbis*: p. 2 (farm) William Gottlieb; *Getty*: Taxi, p. 19; *Image Works*: Jeff Greenberg, p. 5, Geri Engbert, p. 15; *Photo Edit*: Michelle D. Birdwell, p. 7, David Young Wolff, p. 13; *Corbis*: Ariel Skelley, p. 9, Annie Griffiths Bell, p. 11; *Alamy*: f1 online, p. 17; *Superstock*: age footstock, p. 21.

Printed in Malaysia
1 3 5 6 4 2